THE ELEMENTS

Oxygen

John Farndon

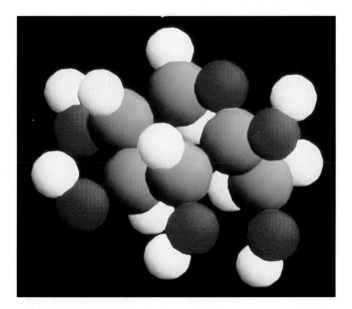

MARSHALL CAVENDISH
NEW YORK

Benchmark Books
Marshall Cavendish Corporation
99 White Plains Road
Tarrytown, New York 10591-9001

Library of Congress Cataloging-in-Publication Data
Farndon, John.
Oxygen / John Farndon.
p.   cm. — (The elements)
Includes index.
Summary: Explores the history of the chemical element oxygen and explains
its chemistry, how it works in the body, and its importance in our lives.
ISBN 0-7614-0879-7 (lib. bdg.)
1. Oxygen—Juvenile literature. [1. Oxygen.] I. Title. II. Series: Elements (Benchmark Books)
QD181.01F36 1999
546'.721—dc21 97-52236 CIP AC

Printed in Hong Kong

Picture credits
Corbis (UK) Ltd: 4, 8, 11, 13, 14, 15, 17, 18.
Images Colour Library: 30.
Science Photo Library: 6, 7, 9, 10, 12, 16, 19, 20, 21, 22, 23, 24, 25, 26, 27.

Series created by Brown Packaging Partworks
Designed by wda

Contents

The air surrounding this freefall parachutist is one-fifth oxygen.

element that it is deeply involved in virtually every major natural process. Anything that burns at all will burn better and brighter in oxygen.

What is oxygen?

Oxygen is the element that makes Earth tick. There is more oxygen on Earth than any other element. It makes up one-fifth of the air around us. We cannot see it, feel it, taste it, or smell it, but we need to breathe it to stay alive. Oxygen reacts so well with almost every other

The oxygen atom

Atoms are the building blocks of elements. They are far too small to see without a powerful microscope—the period at the end of this sentence would cover 250 billion atoms.

At the center of each atom is a nucleus. This contains tiny particles called protons, which have a positive electrical charge. Oxygen has an atomic number of eight, which means it has eight protons.

The nucleus also contains neutrons, which have no charge. Most oxygen atoms have eight neutrons. An oxygen atom with eight protons and eight neutrons is called oxygen-16. But a tiny number of oxygen atoms have extra neutrons. Oxygen-17 has one extra; oxygen-18 has two extra. These variations are called isotopes.

Around the nucleus there are even smaller, negatively charged particles, called electrons. The number of electrons is the same as the number of protons.

Joining in pairs

Oxygen has the chemical formula O, but oxygen atoms are so reactive they rarely survive long by themselves. Most oxygen atoms in the air are combined in pairs called diatomic molecules. These have the formula O_2.

ATOMS AT WORK

The eight electrons of an oxygen atom are arranged in two shells: an inner shell with two electrons and an outer shell with six electrons. Yet atoms are only stable if they have eight electrons in their outer shell.

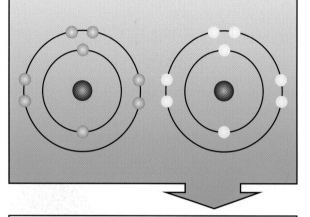

When one oxygen atom meets another, each shares two of its electrons with the other so that both atoms end up with eight electrons. The two atoms become locked together to form a stable molecule.

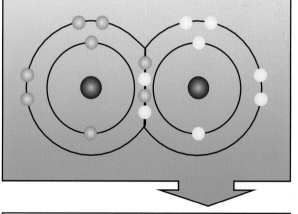

This link-up involves sharing electrons and is called a covalent bond. The bond in an oxygen molecule is called a double bond because it involves two pairs of electrons. The molecule can be written like this:

$$O = O$$

OXYGEN ATOM

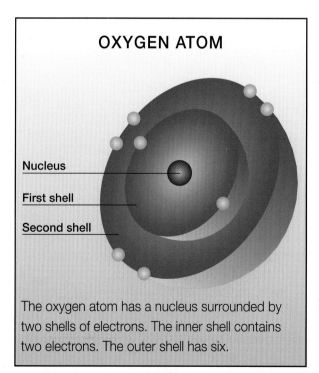

Nucleus

First shell

Second shell

The oxygen atom has a nucleus surrounded by two shells of electrons. The inner shell contains two electrons. The outer shell has six.

Where oxygen is found

Oxygen is the fourth most abundant substance in the universe. It is found in the stars, in nebulae (clouds of gas between stars), and in the Sun.

Oxygen is also by far the most plentiful element on and in Earth's surface. It exists as diatomic oxygen molecules in the air. It exists separately as a gas and in combination with other elements as a solid and a liquid.

Almost half the mass of Earth's crust is made of oxygen atoms, joined with other elements to make rocks. Ninety-eight percent of Earth's crust is silicates—minerals that contain silicon and oxygen.

DID YOU KNOW?

HOW THE AIR GOT ITS OXYGEN

When Earth was young, there was barely any oxygen in the air. Air was a poisonous soup of gases belched out by volcanoes—nitrogen, carbon dioxide, water vapor, and hydrogen.

Unlike the other planets, Earth is just the right temperature for water to exist as a liquid, so the water vapor gradually condensed to create the oceans. Much of the carbon dioxide was dissolved in ocean water and turned into carbonate sediments as fragments of rock settled on the ocean bed. A little oxygen was added to the atmosphere as sunlight split water vapor into hydrogen and oxygen. Oxygen was only added to the air in large quantities when plant life evolved.

Life first appeared on Earth almost four billion years ago. But for a long time, it was only bacteria. However, two billion years ago, a special kind of bacteria called cyanobacteria, or blue-green algae, appeared. These algae were the first plants, and like all green plants they release oxygen as they absorb energy from sunlight. The amount of oxygen each releases is tiny, but there are huge numbers of algae in the oceans, and over a billion years or more they built up the level of oxygen in the air.

This beautiful pink crystal is rose quartz. The chemical name for quartz is silicon oxide. Pure quartz is colorless, but traces of other elements give the crystals different colors

The Martian atmosphere contains only a tiny amount of oxygen compared with Earth's atmosphere.

Water is a combination of light hydrogen atoms with heavy oxygen atoms. So almost 90 percent of the mass of the oceans is oxygen atoms, as well as a similar proportion of the water in rivers, lakes, and clouds.

Atmospheric oxygen

In the atmosphere, oxygen exists on its own as a gas. In fact, 21 percent of the atmosphere's mass is oxygen. The rest is nitrogen, along with small amounts of carbon dioxide and water vapor and traces of a few other gases.

Only Earth, of all the planets in the solar system, has so much oxygen gas in its atmosphere. In comparison, the atmosphere of Mars is less than 0.13 percent oxygen, while that of Venus is less than 0.003 percent oxygen. On these planets, almost all the oxygen is combined with carbon to make carbon dioxide.

How oxygen was discovered

Two hundred or so years ago, most scientists had different ideas about the air and fire. They thought air was just a single gas. They explained fire by the "phlogiston" theory. This was the idea that when anything burned, a special fire substance called phlogiston was involved.

New discoveries

In the 1770s, a number of chemists began to conduct experiments that were to overturn this theory. In 1773, Swedish chemist Carl Scheele (1742–1786) discovered that nitric acid released a gas when heated. Scheele named this gas "fire air" because it burned brightly.

A year later, Englishman Joseph Priestley (1733–1804), probably unaware of Scheele's work, also found the gas by heating mercuric oxide. Priestley saw that it made a candle burn brilliantly. He wrote that "two mice and myself have had the privilege of breathing this air." Later Priestley demonstrated that this gas was given off by plants and that animals died without it.

The significance of oxygen

Yet it was French scientist Antoine Lavoisier who realized the real significance of the gas and showed that it is one of the two main constituents of air. Lavoisier repeated Priestley's experiments in a sealed container. By carefully weighing

English scientist Joseph Priestley discovered a gas that was given off by plants and that animals needed to live. But he did not realize that the gas was one of the main components of air.

French scientist Antoine Lavoisier showed that air is mainly a mixture of the gases oxygen and nitrogen.

DID YOU KNOW?

ANTOINE LAVOISIER

Born in Paris in 1743, Antoine Lavoisier is said to be the "father of modern chemistry." At just 23, he wrote an ingenious essay on how fuels burned in streetlamps, which got him elected to the French Royal Academy of Sciences. He became a tax "farmer" (someone who collects taxes) but involved himself in all kinds of projects, such as improving Paris's water supply, French farming methods, savings banks, and much more. He also conducted a series of brilliant chemistry experiments—not only discovering that air is made of oxygen and nitrogen, but also that water consists of hydrogen and oxygen. Lavoisier was the first to arrange chemicals into family groups and explain why some chemicals form new substances when mixed. Sadly, when the French Revolution came, Lavoisier was guillotined like other tax farmers.

everything, he proved there was no such thing as phlogiston. When the metal burned, he showed, it gained weight simply because it combines with some of the air, not because it absorbed the mysterious phlogiston. (The reaction between a substance and oxygen from air was later termed oxidation.)

He also showed that this part of the air was the same gas as Scheele's "fire air," while the rest of the air was an unburnable gas. Lavoisier named this unburnable gas "azote." Today we know it as nitrogen. It makes up four-fifths of air.

Giving it a name

The honor of giving oxygen its name also belongs to Antoine Lavoisier. He noticed that the fire gas tended to form acids when it combined with certain substances. He named the fire gas "oxygen," from the Greek words *oxys* meaning "acid" and *genos* meaning "forming."

Special characteristics

Oxygen is a gas at all normal temperatures and pressures. It does not begin to condense (turn to liquid) until the temperature has dropped far below the coldest temperatures that ever occur naturally on Earth. It condenses to a pale blue liquid at −297.4°F (−183°C), and a solid at about −361°F (−218.4°C).

Oxygen's boiling point, however, is marginally higher than nitrogen's. This slight difference allows oxygen to be extracted from the air, which is essentially a mixture of nitrogen and oxygen, by liquefying it.

The process involves bringing the temperature of the air down by alternately compressing and expanding it in pressure-

DID YOU KNOW?

ROCKET FUEL

Liquid oxygen was the fuel that sent men to the Moon and brought them back. It is also the fuel that powers the main engines of the space shuttle. Launching a spacecraft out beyond the pull of Earth's gravity requires huge amounts of power, and this is usually achieved with liquid fuel rockets.

Liquid fuel rockets have two tanks, one containing LOX (liquid oxygen) and the other liquid hydrogen. When these are mixed and ignited in the rocket's combustion chamber, they expand with such ferocity that the rocket is propelled upward with awesome power. The fuel burns to produce an exhaust of water vapor.

Unlike solid rocket fuels, LOX and hydrogen must be stored in special containers at very low temperatures and handled with extreme care, but they provide matchless power for the launch vehicles that send spacecraft into space.

sealed flasks. When the temperature of the air drops to almost −328°F (−200°C), it turns to liquid.

The oxygen is then separated from the air by distilling it, that is, by boiling it off and taking the condensation at different levels. The oxygen that is removed from the air can be stored as a liquid, called LOX, at normal temperatures in strong metal pressurized containers.

Liquid oxygen supplied the power that sent the first astronauts to the Moon.

How oxygen reacts

Oxygen is among the most reactive of all elements. The smallness of its atom, and the two electrons "missing" from the atom's outer shell (see page 5), mean that oxygen is more willing to join with other atoms and form compounds than virtually any other element.

In fact, oxygen reacts to form compounds with almost every element. The only ones it does not combine with are helium, neon, argon, krypton, and fluorine. It will also react with a huge range of compounds and take the place of other elements to form new combinations.

Compounds of an element with oxygen are called oxides. They are often made by heating or burning the element, or a compound of it, in air or oxygen.

Metal oxides

When metals combine with oxygen, they generally form solid crystals. Magnesium oxide, for example, is the white powder, or crystals, called magnesia. This is used in treatments for indigestion or mixed with magnesium chloride to make "stucco," the white cement used to decorate buildings.

Metal oxides are usually ionic compounds. In ionic compounds, the atoms of one element donate their outer electrons to the atoms of the other

The ornate decoration on this arch in Spain is stucco, a cement that contains an oxygen compound.

element. The metal atoms lose electrons to become positively charged ions, while the oxygen atoms gain electrons to become negatively charged ions. The difference in the electrical charge bonds the metal and oxygen ions together.

Nonmetal oxides

Nonmetals generally form covalent compounds with oxygen. In covalent compounds, the atoms of the elements do not donate electrons but share them. This means the atoms must always be together, so this type of bond creates a molecule.

Typically, these oxides are very volatile and form strong acids when dissolved in

ALUMINA—RUBIES AND SAPPHIRES

Aluminum oxide, or alumina, occurs in two main forms: alpha-alumina and gamma-alumina. Gamma-alumina reacts with acids and bases but alpha-alumina is weakly acidic, so it is resistant to acid attack.

Alpha-alumina is one of the hardest materials known; only diamond and silicon carbide are harder. It can be extracted industrially from bauxite ore, and because of its toughness, resistance to acid attack, and high melting point, it is used to line blast furnaces, as well as for ceramics. But alpha-alumina also occurs naturally as the mineral corundum, which is ground to a powder for sharpening knives or coated on to paper to sand down metals. In certain forms, corundum is a beautiful, precious gem. Minute traces of chromium turn crystals of corundum into the red gem ruby. Traces of titanium turn them into sapphire.

running cars. Most of these reactions involve either oxidation or reduction.

Originally, oxidation just meant that a substance was gaining oxygen, while reduction meant that it was losing oxygen. But this is just part of a wider picture of important reactions, so the terms have been extended. When a substance simply

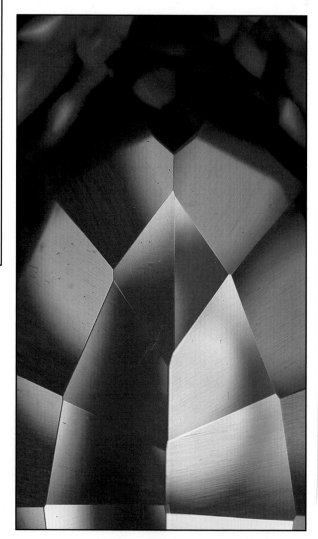

The mineral corundum contains aluminum and oxygen. Tiny specks of the metal titanium turn the mineral into the beautiful blue gemstone sapphire.

water. Power stations, for instance, release huge quantities of nitrogen oxide and sulfur dioxide into the atmosphere.

When these oxides dissolve in the moisture from the air, they form nitric and sulfuric acids. These are the acids that fall as acid rain, damaging trees, water life, and buildings.

Oxidation and reduction

Oxygen reactions are involved in a huge range of everyday processes, from keeping living things alive to cooking food and

Power stations produce dirty fumes of nitrogen oxide and sulfur oxide, which create smog.

loses hydrogen, that too is oxidation, whether it involves oxygen or not; when it gains hydrogen, that is reduction.

Transferring electrons

Since the loss or gain of oxygen by any substance involves the movement of electrons between atoms, scientists now use the terms oxidation and reduction to describe any reaction involving the transfer of electrons. Atoms that lose electrons are said to be oxidized and atoms that gain electrons are said to be reduced, even when oxygen plays no part.

Any substance that either donates oxygen or electrons or accepts hydrogen and so causes oxidation is called an oxidizing agent. Substances such as these

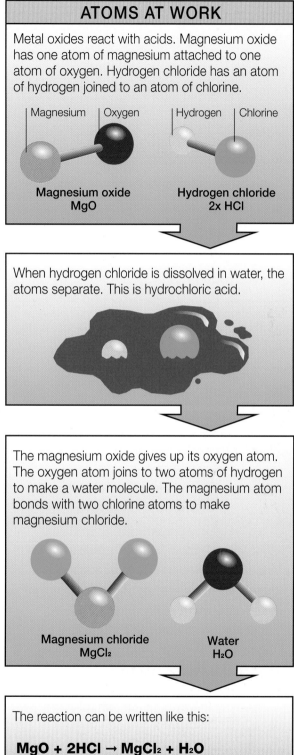

ATOMS AT WORK

Metal oxides react with acids. Magnesium oxide has one atom of magnesium attached to one atom of oxygen. Hydrogen chloride has an atom of hydrogen joined to an atom of chlorine.

Magnesium | Oxygen   Hydrogen | Chlorine

Magnesium oxide MgO   **Hydrogen chloride** 2x HCl

When hydrogen chloride is dissolved in water, the atoms separate. This is hydrochloric acid.

The magnesium oxide gives up its oxygen atom. The oxygen atom joins to two atoms of hydrogen to make a water molecule. The magnesium atom bonds with two chlorine atoms to make magnesium chloride.

Magnesium chloride MgCl₂   **Water** H₂O

The reaction can be written like this:

MgO + 2HCl → MgCl₂ + H₂O

The number of atoms of each element is the same on both sides of the equation.

usually contain plenty of oxygen. Any substance that donates electrons and so causes reduction is a reducing agent.

Everyday uses

Oxidation and reduction are seen in a huge number of everyday situations—when things burn, when metals rust, when animals breathe and move, when plants grow, and much more besides.

Bleaching, for instance, is an oxidation process. Household bleaches contain the oxygen-rich substance hydrogen peroxide, which is a powerful oxidizing agent. When

This police officer is testing a driver's breath to see if he has been drinking. The test is based on the reaction between oxygen and alcohol.

bleach is put on colored clothes, the bleach oxidizes the dyes, and this reaction robs them of their color.

The breathalyzer used for testing drunk drivers involves oxidation, too. Alcohol in the driver's breath is oxidized in the breathalyzer into ethanoic acid, which triggers an electric current. The strength of the current varies with the amount of ethanoic acid, so this reveals how much alcohol there is in the driver's breath.

Preventing oxidation

With so much oxygen in the air, oxidation occurs all too often when it is not wanted—metals rust and tarnish, fruit goes brown, and fatty food turns bad.

Metals and foods, therefore, are often treated to prevent oxidation. Antioxidants,

---

DID YOU KNOW?

RUST AND TARNISH

When exposed to air, most metals oxidize at the surface, forming a coating or tarnish of dull metal oxide. With aluminum and silver, the tarnish shields the untarnished metal from the air and prevents further corrosion. With iron and steel, however, exposure to air causes rust. Rusting is an oxidation process, forming brown iron oxide. But the oxide layer does not shield the uncorroded metal, it simply crumbles away. Air and moisture can reach the lower layers, and rust can quickly eat through the metal. The only way to prevent rusting is to apply a protective coating to stop the air reaching the metal. Paints and varnishes help prevent rusting. Galvanizing (coating with zinc) is more effective, but also more expensive.

for example, are often added to fatty foods and oils because fats are very ready to oxidize. The antioxidant takes their place and oxidizes instead.

The reaction with oxygen in air has made these apples turn rotten and brown.

ATOMS AT WORK

Hydrogen peroxide is a good oxidizing agent because it readily gives up its oxygen to other elements. One molecule of hydrogen peroxide has two oxygen atoms and two hydrogen atoms.

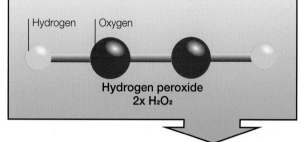

Hydrogen   Oxygen

Hydrogen peroxide
2x H_2O_2

If hydrogen peroxide is left standing for a long time, the molecules decompose (fall apart). This occurs more quickly if oxygen, metals, or specks of dirt are present. It is also speeded up if the hydrogen peroxide is heated.

The atoms join together in a different combination to give molecules of water and oxygen.

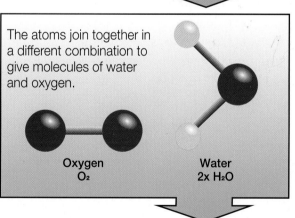

Oxygen
O_2

Water
2x H_2O

When hydrogen peroxide decomposes, a chemical reaction takes place. This can be written like this:

$$2H_2O_2 \rightarrow 2H_2O + O_2$$

This shows us that two molecules of hydrogen peroxide produce two molecules of water and one molecule of oxygen.

Combustion

Combustion means burning, and it is one of the most important of all chemical reactions. It gives us warmth in fires, heats food on a gas "cooker," generates electricity in many power stations, provides the power for engines in cars, trains, jet planes, and rockets, and gives energy to our bodies and the bodies of every mammal on Earth.

Fuels and burning

Combustion is defined as an exothermic reaction—that is, one that creates heat and light. It takes place between a substance called a fuel and a gas. Other gases such as chlorine can be involved, but the gas is usually oxygen from the air and the reaction is an oxidation reaction.

Sometimes the oxidation reaction is slow as it is when sugar burns in our bodies to release energy or when charcoal glows on a barbecue. Sometimes it is faster, and the fuel bursts into flames, as when paper or wood burns. Occasionally the reaction is so rapid that huge amounts of heat are created very quickly—too quickly for it all to be dispersed easily. The result is an explosion, as when dynamite is ignited.

Substances burn in oxygen with a distinctive color. Magnesium produces a bright white flame.

FLAME FACTS

Different substances burn in oxygen with a different colored flame:

- carbon glows bright red and yellow
- hydrogen burns blue
- magnesium burns bright white
- sodium burns bright yellow
- sulfur burns bright blue
- zinc burns bright azure (light blue)

Ignition

Fuels only burn when they have reached a certain temperature, called the ignition temperature. This is fortunate; without the ignition temperature, things would be bursting into flames all the time!

To set something on fire, we must first raise it to the ignition temperature, perhaps by setting a match or a spark to it. This heat provides energy called "activation energy," which gets the particles in the substance moving fast enough to react with oxygen.

DID YOU KNOW?

FOSSIL FUELS

Most of the fuels we use today are fossil fuels—coal, oil, and natural gas. The fossil fuels are the remains of living creatures, which have been transformed into fuels in the ground over millions of years. These substances are called hydrocarbons, because their main constituents are hydrogen and carbon. So when they are burned, two oxidation reactions take place. In one, the carbon in the fuel joins with oxygen in the air to create carbon dioxide. In the other, the hydrogen joins with oxygen to create water.

This controlled fire is in New Mexico. The grass around a cluster of pine trees is being burned to protect local houses. The orange blaze is the result of a reaction between carbon in the grass and oxygen in the air.

Combustion needs a gas

Sometimes, a solid fuel will react directly with oxygen in the air, and all we see is a glow. When we see a flame, it is because the heat has vaporized some of the fuel so that the combustion takes place between oxygen and another gas.

In fact, most of the things we burn, whether they are solid fuels such as coal or liquid fuels such as paraffin, must be turned into gas before they will burn.

The match or spark that starts a fire provides just enough heat to turn some of the fuel into gas and get the burning process going. With coal, though, you may need to heat it for some time to release enough gas to start the fire. Once the fire is burning properly, the heat from the burning gas is enough to create more gases and keep the process going.

Even the most explosive combinations of gases, such as oxygen and hydrogen, do not always react instantly. Even here, you need a spark. This is because most of the hydrogen and oxygen atoms are tied up safely in molecules. The spark releases hydrogen atoms from their molecules, so they start to break up oxygen molecules.

This firefighter is using foam to put out a chemical blaze. The foam covers the burning material, cutting it off from the oxygen in the air. When the oxygen supply is no longer available, the fire dies out.

DID YOU KNOW?

PUTTING OUT FIRES

Fires will not burn if they are starved of oxygen. So the best way to put out a fire is to cut off its oxygen supply. Dowsing a fire with water, smothering it with a fire blanket, or covering it with foam from a fire extinguisher all do this.

FIRE EXTINGUISHERS ARE OF THREE MAIN TYPES:

● Water, propelled by pressurized carbon dioxide. These should never be used if the fire is burning fat or oil or if there is any danger from electricity.
● Carbon dioxide foam and gas smothers the fire. This is usually kept in pressurized black metal cylinders.
● Dry powder extinguishers use a powder of hydrogen carbonate, pumped out of the canister by pressurized carbon dioxide. Old fire extinguishers used soda acid, which created carbon dioxide when sodium carbonate and an acid reacted together.

Oxygen and life

Life depends on oxygen. Oxygen is involved in all the processes that keep our bodies going, and we must breathe it from the air continuously to stay alive. If the brain is starved of oxygen for even a minute, it is damaged beyond repair.

Oxygen is essential to the existence of every single cell in the body. Just as a fire only burns if there is plenty of air, so each cell needs oxygen to burn up the food it receives from the blood and release the energy locked within. The process by which this occurs is cellular respiration.

Food arrives at the cell in the form of a chemical called glucose, a form of sugar. When glucose is burned in the cell to release its energy, the hydrogen in it combines with the oxygen to make water, while the carbon combines with it to make carbon dioxide. The carbon dioxide is useless and has to be removed. This is what happens when we breathe out.

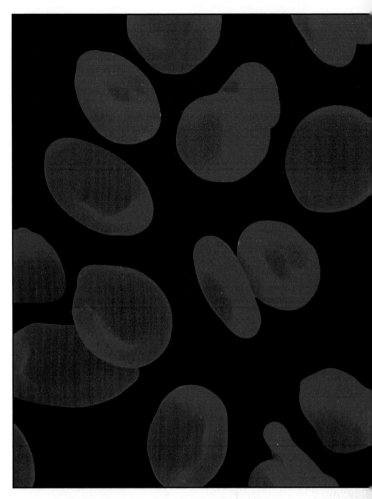

Red blood cells transport oxygen around the body. The cells contain a compound called hemoglobin, which binds to the oxygen and carries it along.

Moving round the body

Oxygen enters our bodies as we breathe air into the lungs. Each lung has thousands of branch-like passages, which are covered with tiny blood vessels. These tiny blood vessels have very thin walls. As blood washes over the lungs through the blood vessels, oxygen seeps from the air inside the lungs through the lining of the lungs and into the blood.

The oxygen is swept away by the blood's circulation and quickly delivered to every part of the body. Remarkably, it takes less than 90 seconds, on average, for blood to circulate oxygen around the entire body, though it takes a few seconds to get it to the heart and brain and a few minutes to get it to the feet.

Oxygen carriers

Oxygen is not just swept along in the blood. Instead it is stowed safely inside buttoned-shaped red blood cells. Each red cell can carry a great deal of oxygen because it contains a special substance called hemoglobin. Hemoglobin has a unique relationship with oxygen. When there is plenty of oxygen around, it combines readily with the hemoglobin. When there is little oxygen present, hemoglobin quickly releases its oxygen, so the oxygen is dropped off wherever it is needed. Hemoglobin also helps carry the unwanted carbon dioxide away.

When carrying oxygen, hemoglobin glows bright scarlet. But when the oxygen is released, the hemoglobin fades to dull purple and the color of the blood fades with it. Deoxygenated blood on the way back to the lungs is a deep purply red. If the body is deprived of oxygen, this plum-colored blood turns the skin almost blue.

This child has been poisoned by carbon monoxide. He is breathing pure oxygen so that his red blood cells can quickly become charged with oxygen.

DID YOU KNOW?

CARBON MONOXIDE POISONING

Carbon monoxide in car exhausts has no smell but it is a deadly poison. Its effect on the body is devastating because it prevents the blood from carrying oxygen around the body. When hemoglobin combines with oxygen to make oxyhemoglobin, it is quite ready to release its load of oxygen when needed, thus freeing the hemoglobin to carry more oxygen. But when carbon monoxide combines with hemoglobin to form carboxyhemoglobin, the link is not easily broken, so oxygen transport is blocked. If only 10 percent of your body's hemoglobin is tied up in carboxyhemoglobin, you will get a bad headache. If any more is tied up, it can be fatal.

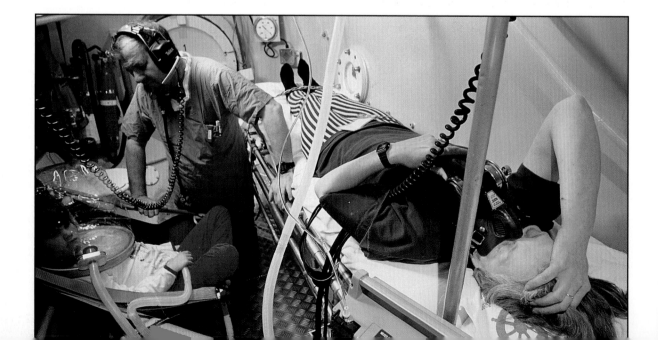

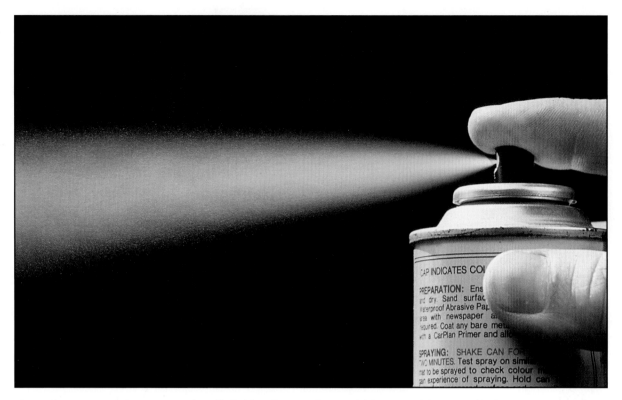

Aerosol sprays contain compounds called chlorofluorocarbons, which react with ozone in the upper atmosphere.

Ozone

Most of the oxygen in and around Earth occurs as molecules consisting of two oxygen atoms. This is called diatomic oxygen. But oxygen can exist in several different forms, called allotropes. Oxygen's other form is triatomic oxygen, in which three oxygen atoms are bonded together to make the molecule.

Triatomic oxygen or trioxygen is better known as ozone. Ordinary dioxygen is colorless, but ozone is light blue in color. It also has a distinct, slightly pungent smell. Ozone is heavier than dioxygen and condenses at a much higher temperature to form a dark blue liquid. It is soluble in water, but it cannot be used in the body.

How ozone forms

Dioxygen can be turned into ozone by passing an electrical current through it. This is how ozone is made in industry.

Ozone commonly results from automobile exhausts and industrial fumes. When nitrogen oxides from the fumes are caught in sunlight, they are converted by the light into ozone.

This reaction not only fills the air with a thick haze called petrochemical smog but pollutes it with poisonous ozone, which

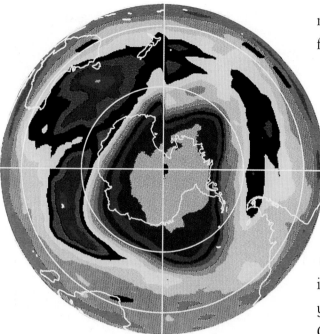

The pink oval shape in this satellite picture shows the hole in the ozone layer over the South Pole.

makes breathing difficult. Some scientists believe ozone created this way is partly responsible for acid rain.

Ozone occurs naturally in the atmosphere where high-energy ultraviolet sunlight bombards oxygen molecules and converts them into ozone. All this ozone is concentrated in the stratosphere, 9 to 12½ miles (15 to 21 km) above the ground, and this layer soaks up most of this high-energy sunlight.

CFCs

The ozone layer is being attacked by pollution. Human-made gases called chlorofluorocarbons or CFCs are used in aerosol sprays and refrigerators and to manufacture the foam plastics that make fast-food packages.

When they were developed in the 1930s, CFCs were thought to be a wonder gas, for they appeared completely inert— odorless, nontoxic, nonflammable, and unreactive with just about everything. Unfortunately, this very unreactivity has proved to be the problem.

When they are released into the atmosphere, CFCs drift slowly upward into the stratosphere over about eight years, unaffected by the surrounding air. Once there, they can survive for a century or more. But they are gradually broken down by ultraviolet rays from the Sun, releasing chlorine atoms.

The chlorine atoms react with the ozone, converting it into oxygen. The chlorine only acts as a catalyst, making the reaction go faster; it does not change itself. So the chlorine atoms survive to destroy thousands of ozone molecules.

Thinning ozone

Ozone is spread so thinly through the air that if it was squeezed into one layer, it would be only a little thicker than an orange peel. But without this fragile layer, life on Earth would be destroyed by ultraviolet radiation from the Sun.

Any thinning of the ozone layer as a result of CFCs could therefore have grave consequences. A major reduction in the

Ozone helps to protect us from the Sun's ultraviolet rays, which cause sunburn and other skin problems.

ozone layer could bring a whole host of problems for plants and animals.

Every spring, holes in the ozone layer naturally appear over the North and South poles, where the atmosphere is at its shallowest. Satellite pictures show that these holes are getting bigger every year and taking longer to close up.

In June 1990, representatives of 93 nations, including the United States, agreed to phase out production of CFCs and other ozone enemies. But huge quantities are still being used, even though they are now rare in aerosols. Meanwhile, those CFCs that are already in the stratosphere are eating away at the ozone layer, and they will continue to do so for at least a century.

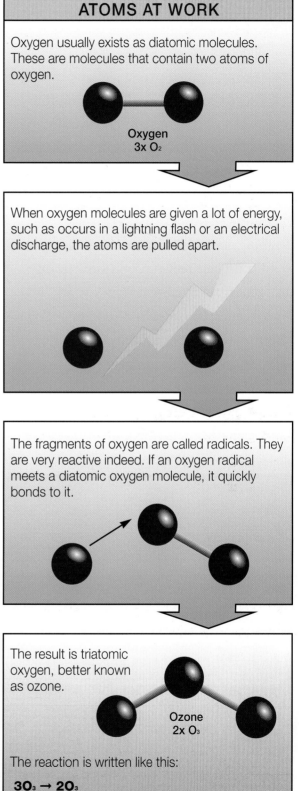

ATOMS AT WORK

Oxygen usually exists as diatomic molecules. These are molecules that contain two atoms of oxygen.

Oxygen
$3x\ O_2$

When oxygen molecules are given a lot of energy, such as occurs in a lightning flash or an electrical discharge, the atoms are pulled apart.

The fragments of oxygen are called radicals. They are very reactive indeed. If an oxygen radical meets a diatomic oxygen molecule, it quickly bonds to it.

The result is triatomic oxygen, better known as ozone.

Ozone
$2x\ O_3$

The reaction is written like this:

$$3O_2 \rightarrow 2O_3$$

The oxygen cycle

The amount of oxygen in and around Earth is fixed. But this oxygen is fed again and again through the world's living systems in a never-ending circle called the oxygen cycle. Our needs are just part of this cycle. The cycle involves a continual exchange of gases between the air and animals and plants.

In a process called respiration, animals and plants take oxygen from air and give back carbon dioxide. In a process called photosynthesis, plants take carbon dioxide from air and water and give back oxygen. Respiration and photosynthesis are effectively opposite processes. Respiration is an oxidation reaction, which takes oxygen from the air or from water. Photosynthesis is a reduction reaction; it adds oxygen gas to the air.

Respiration

Respiration is the complex series of chemical reactions in which oxygen is used to burn sugars and produce energy. Carbon dioxide and water form as waste products. Usually the reaction is helped along by catalysts called enzymes.

Taking the oxygen

Different organisms get the oxygen they need for respiration in different ways. Plants and simple creatures absorb it directly from air and water through cell walls. Fish pass water through gills, while large land animals breathe air into lungs. Larger creatures circulate oxygen through their bodies in the blood, fish taking it in from water passed over gills and land creatures from air breathed into lungs.

Photosynthesis

In photosynthesis, plants take in carbon dioxide and water and convert them into foods called carbohydrates. The reaction needs sunlight and a catalyst called chlorophyll, the substance that makes leaves green, to take place.

Green plants take carbon dioxide from the air and release oxygen back to the air.

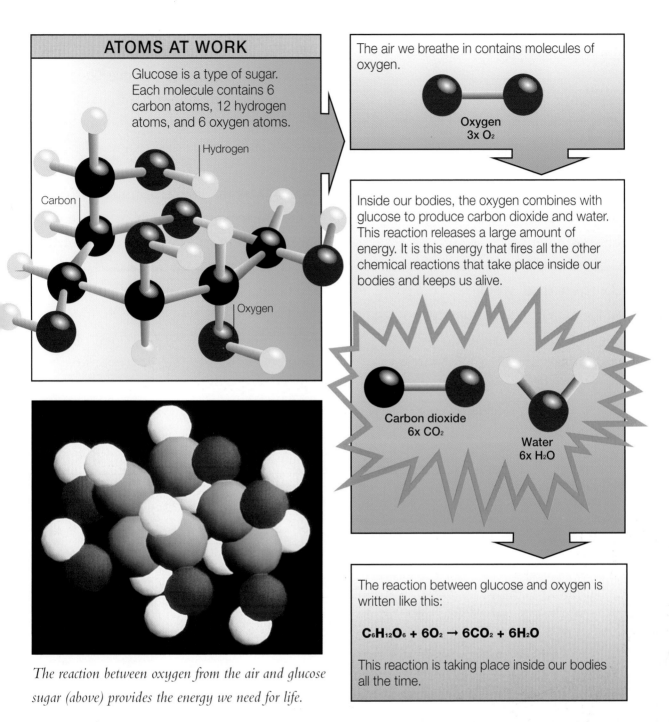

ATOMS AT WORK

Glucose is a type of sugar. Each molecule contains 6 carbon atoms, 12 hydrogen atoms, and 6 oxygen atoms.

Hydrogen

Carbon

Oxygen

The air we breathe in contains molecules of oxygen.

Oxygen
3x O_2

Inside our bodies, the oxygen combines with glucose to produce carbon dioxide and water. This reaction releases a large amount of energy. It is this energy that fires all the other chemical reactions that take place inside our bodies and keeps us alive.

Carbon dioxide
6x CO_2

Water
6x H_2O

The reaction between glucose and oxygen is written like this:

$$C_6H_{12}O_6 + 6O_2 \rightarrow 6CO_2 + 6H_2O$$

This reaction is taking place inside our bodies all the time.

The reaction between oxygen from the air and glucose sugar (above) provides the energy we need for life.

Enormous quantities of oxygen are taken in by plants and animals every day, and huge quantities of oxygen are returned to the air by plants. The astonishing thing is that these amounts exactly balance so that overall the amount of oxygen in the air stays the same. No one knows quite why this is, but it is fortunate that it does, for we would soon feel ill in air that is starved of oxygen.

How oxygen is used

Oxygen from the air is used by all of us all of the time for staying alive and in innumerable processes both natural and artificial. But it is also bottled industrially and used pure in a whole range of other processes.

Oxygen and steel

By far the largest consumer of bottled oxygen is the steel industry. The basic oxygen process is the method used to manufacture most of the world's steel. Steel is made from iron in two stages. The first involves removing impurities from the iron. The second involves adding alloy materials. It is in the first stage that oxygen is used.

In an enormous container called a converter, all the impurities are burned out of the molten steel with a blast of oxygen, bubbled through it down a water-cooled pipe. This takes out all the carbon dioxide and other nonmetals in a much more rapid and controllable way than if air was used. For each 13 tons (12 tonnes) of steel, about 1.1 tons (1 tonne) of gaseous oxygen

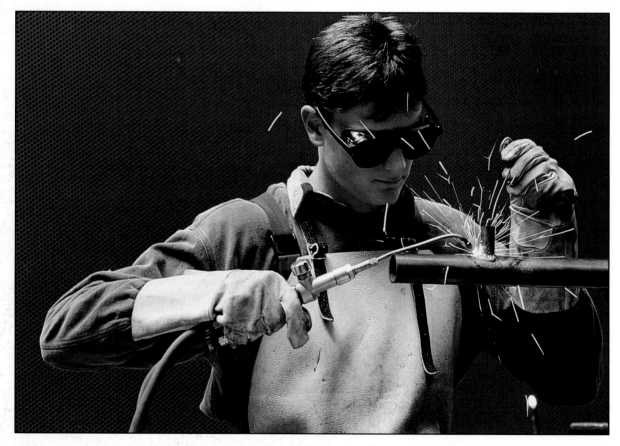

An oxyacetylene torch generates temperatures that are high enough to melt metals.

is needed. The unwanted fumes are funnelled off to a gas cleaning plant. After a while, samples of the steel are taken for analysis, and then alloys are added to make the finished material.

Lifesaving oxygen

Bottled oxygen provides immediate oxygen for people to breathe in a variety of life-threatening situations. It is used in hospitals to give patients an oxygen boost when their bodies are unable to take it quickly or well enough from the air.

Climbers use oxygen on top of high mountains, where the air is very thin, and divers have oxygen tanks under the water where oxygen is scarce. It is used in airplanes, submarines, diving bells, spacecraft, and other confined spaces where the air's own oxygen would soon be used up.

Other uses

Many kinds of welding and cutting apparatus rely on the high temperatures possible with "oxy-gas" flames. The very high temperatures that can be reached with oxygen also help with waste incineration. Other uses include sewage treatment and rocket fuels.

Humans need oxygen to breathe. People, such as deep-sea divers, who go to places where oxygen is not available have to carry their own supply.

Periodic table

Everything in the universe is made from combinations of substances called elements. Elements are the building blocks of matter. They are made of tiny atoms, which are much too small to see.

The character of an atom depends on how many even tinier particles called protons there are in its center, or nucleus. An element's atomic number is the same as the number of protons.

Scientists have found around 110 different elements. About 90 elements occur naturally on Earth. The rest have been made in experiments.

All these elements are set out on a chart called the periodic table. This lists all the elements in order according to their atomic number.

The elements at the left of the table are metals. Those at the right are nonmetals. Between the metals and the nonmetals are the metalloids, which sometimes act like metals and sometimes like nonmetals.

- On the left of the table are the alkali metals. These elements have just one electron in their outer shells.

- On the right of the periodic table are the noble gases. These elements have full outer shells.

- Elements in the same group have the same number of electrons in their outer shells.

- Elements get more reactive as you go down a group.

- The number of electrons orbiting the nucleus increases down each group.

- The transition metals are in the middle of the table, between Groups II and III.

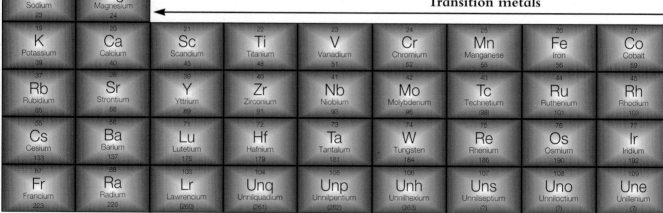

Group I

Group II

Transition metals

1 **H** Hydrogen 1								
3 **Li** Lithium 7	4 **Be** Beryllium 9							
11 **Na** Sodium 23	12 **Mg** Magnesium 24							
19 **K** Potassium 39	20 **Ca** Calcium 40	21 **Sc** Scandium 45	22 **Ti** Titanium 48	23 **V** Vanadium 51	24 **Cr** Chromium 52	25 **Mn** Manganese 55	26 **Fe** Iron 56	27 **Co** Cobalt 59
37 **Rb** Rubidium 85	38 **Sr** Strontium 88	39 **Y** Yttrium 89	40 **Zr** Zirconium 91	41 **Nb** Niobium 93	42 **Mo** Molybdenum 96	43 **Tc** Technetium (98)	44 **Ru** Ruthenium 101	45 **Rh** Rhodium 103
55 **Cs** Cesium 133	56 **Ba** Barium 137	71 **Lu** Lutetium 175	72 **Hf** Hafnium 179	73 **Ta** Tantalum 181	74 **W** Tungsten 184	75 **Re** Rhenium 186	76 **Os** Osmium 190	77 **Ir** Iridium 192
87 **Fr** Francium 223	88 **Ra** Radium 226	103 **Lr** Lawrencium (260)	104 **Unq** Unnilquadium (261)	105 **Unp** Unnilpentium (262)	106 **Unh** Unnilhexium (263)	107 **Uns** Unnilseptium (?)	108 **Uno** Unniloctium (?)	109 **Une** Unnilennium (?)

Lanthanide elements

57 **La** Lanthanum 39	58 **Ce** Cerium 140	59 **Pr** Praseodymium 141	60 **Nd** Neodymium 144	61 **Pm** Promethium (145)
89 **Ac** Actinium 227	90 **Th** Thorium 232	91 **Pa** Protactinium 231	92 **U** Uranium 238	93 **Np** Neptunium (237)

Actinide elements

The horizontal rows are called periods. As you go across a period, the atomic number increases by one from each element to the next. The vertical columns are called groups. Elements get heavier as you go down a group. All the elements in a group have the same number of electrons in their outer shells. This means they react in similar ways.

The transition metals fall between Groups II and III. Their electron shells fill up in an unusual way. The lanthanide elements and the actinide elements are set apart from the main table to make it easier to read. All the lanthanide elements and the actinide elements are quite rare.

Oxygen in the table

Oxygen is found on the right hand side of the periodic table among the nonmetals. It has an atomic number of eight, which tells us there are eight protons and eight electrons inside each atom. Oxygen is one of the most reactive elements. It will form compounds with almost every other element in the table.

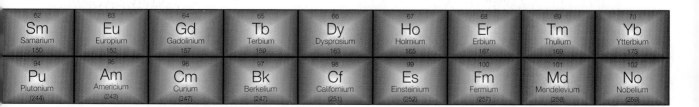

29

Chemical reactions

Chemical reactions are going on all the time—candles burn, nails rust, food is digested. Some reactions involve just two substances; others many more. But whenever a reaction takes place, at least one substance is changed.

In a chemical reaction, the atoms do not change. An iron atom remains an iron atom; an oxygen atom remains an oxygen

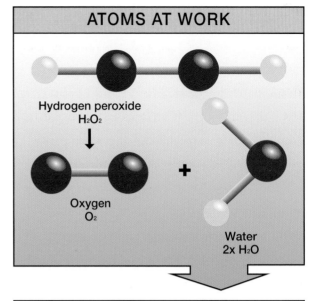

ATOMS AT WORK

Hydrogen peroxide
H_2O_2

Oxygen
O_2

+

Water
$2x H_2O$

The chemical reaction that takes place when hydrogen peroxide decomposes looks like this:

$$2H_2O_2 \rightarrow 2H_2O + O_2$$

This tells us that two molecules of hydrogen peroxide produce two molecules of water and one molecule of oxygen.

Hydrogen peroxide has many uses. It is used to bleach cloth, leather, hair, and paper.

atom. But they join together in different combinations to form new molecules.

Writing an equation

Equations are a quick way of showing what happens in a chemical reaction. They show the atoms and molecules at the beginning and the end of the reaction.

When the number of each atom on both sides of the equation is equal, the equation is balanced. If it is not equal, something must be wrong. So we have to look at the equation again and adjust the number of atoms involved until the equation balances.

Glossary

acid rain: When certain gases rise into the atmosphere, they dissolve in rainwater, making the rain acidic.

allotropes: Different forms of the same elements in which the atoms are arranged in a different pattern.

atmosphere: The layer of air around Earth made of nitrogen, oxygen, carbon dioxide, water vapor, and tiny traces of other gases.

atom: The smallest part of an element that still has all the properties of that element.

atomic number: The number of protons in an atom.

bond: The attraction between two atoms that holds the atoms together.

catalyst: Something that makes a chemical reaction occur more quickly.

chlorofluorocarbons: Artificially made gases, used in aerosols and refrigerators, that damage the ozone layer.

combustion: The chemical reaction between a fuel and a gas (usually oxygen) that is better known as burning.

electron: A tiny particle with a negative charge. Electrons are found inside atoms, where they move around the nucleus in layers called electron shells.

isotopes: Atoms of an element with the same number of protons and electrons but different numbers of neutrons.

metal: An element on the left of the periodic table. Metals are good conductors of heat and electricity.

mineral: A compound or element as it is found in its natural form in Earth.

molecule: A particle that contains atoms held together by chemical bonds.

nebula: A cloud of gas and dust that exists in the spaces between stars.

neutron: A tiny particle with no electrical charge found in the nucleus of an atom.

nonmetal: An element at the right hand side of the periodic table. Nonmetals are liquids or gases at normal temperatures. They are poor at conducting heat and electricity.

nucleus: The center of an atom. It contains protons and neutrons.

oxidation: A reaction in which oxygen is added to something.

ozone: A form of oxygen in which three oxygen atoms join together in a molecule.

periodic table: A chart of all the chemical elements laid out in order of their atomic number.

products: The substances formed in a chemical reaction.

proton: A tiny particle with a positive charge. Protons are found inside the nucleus of an atom.

reactants: The substances that react together in a chemical reaction.

reduction: A reaction in which a substance loses oxygen.

Index